Finding *Peace* in the *Chaos*

A MOM'S SPIRITUAL JOURNEY
52 WEEK DEVOTIONAL

For Bulk Order requests email: contact@adventuresofpookie.com

Printed in the United States of America
Paperback ISBN : 979-8-9988824-1-8
Hardcover ISBN: 979-8-9988824-0-1

www.AdventuresOfPookie.com

Dedication

To my mother, Kelly. You are the embodiment of unconditional love. You've guided me in my best moments and loved me in my worst. You've passed down a love of baking and a heart for helping others, but most of all, you showed me who God truly is. You worked tirelessly, even when you thought no one was watching, and your example has shaped me into the woman I am today. I am forever grateful for your strength, your kindness, and the unwavering love you've always given.

To my bonus mom, Judy. Your prayers for your daughter and step-daughters are a constant reminder of God's faithfulness. Your gentle spirit and steadfast faith remind us all that He is always with us, and your love and wisdom have enriched my life in countless ways.

To my mother-in-law, Audrey. From the moment I entered your family, you welcomed me with open arms and an open heart. Your love for your family is a beautiful example of grace and selflessness, and it inspires me every day. I am so thankful for the warmth and love you've shown me.

Introduction

Motherhood is beautiful—but it's also loud, messy, and relentless. The to-do lists never end. The laundry multiplies. The emotions—yours and theirs—swell like waves. Some days you feel like you're barely holding it together. Other days, you wonder if you're doing any of it right. And yet, right in the middle of the chaos, God whispers: *Peace. My peace is for you.*

This book isn't about having it all figured out or finally becoming the "calm mom" you've always wanted to be. It's about meeting Jesus in your real life—the one with crumbs on the floor, mismatched socks, and prayers whispered between carpool runs. These 52 devotions are here to remind you that peace isn't found in perfection. It's found in a Person. A Savior who steps into your mess, lifts what's heavy, and gently restores your soul.

You won't always feel peaceful. But through God's Word, His presence, and His unfailing love, you can return to peace again and again. So take a deep breath. You're not alone. He's right here, offering rest for your weary heart—and hope for every ordinary, holy day ahead.

Peace THAT DOESN'T MAKE SENSE

SCRIPTURE

"And the peace of God, which transcends all understanding, will guard your hearts and your minds in Christ Jesus." – Philippians 4:7 (NIV)

DEVOTIONAL

Sometimes the noise in our lives isn't just loud—it's relentless. The chaos of parenting, housework, schedules, and emotional strain can leave us gasping for just one moment of silence. But the peace of God isn't about silence. It's about presence.

God's peace shows up not after the storm, but in the middle of it.

You may not be able to control the noise around you, but you can choose where your heart rests. God invites you to sit with Him, even in the mess, and let His peace guard your heart like a shield.

PRAYER

Father, I need Your peace—peace that doesn't depend on circumstances. Help me to pause and breathe in Your presence. Guard my heart and mind when everything feels out of control. Let me feel You near, even when nothing makes sense. Amen.

REFLECTION

Where do you tend to look for peace—quiet moments, fixed problems, a clean house? What would it look like to seek God's peace right where you are?

_____

_____

_____

_____

_____

_____

_____

_____

_____

_____

WHEN YOU FEEL LIKE YOU'RE *Failing*

SCRIPTURE

"My grace is sufficient for you, for my power is made perfect in weakness." – 2 Corinthians 12:9 (NIV)

DEVOTIONAL

We all have those days—when the yelling gets loud, the laundry piles up, and you question if you're doing anything right. In the chaos, guilt sneaks in. But grace does too.

God is not measuring your worth by your performance. He is meeting you in your weakness with power and love. Peace doesn't come from getting it all right—it comes from knowing you're not expected to.

You're allowed to be a work in progress. His grace covers your gaps.

PRAYER

Jesus, I feel like I'm not enough sometimes. Thank You for reminding me that I don't have to be— because You are. Help me to rest in Your grace instead of my own effort. Let peace settle into my heart, even on my messiest days. Amen.

REFLECTION

What is one area where you feel like you're not measuring up? How can you remind yourself of God's grace there today?

_____

_____

_____

_____

_____

_____

_____

_____

_____

_____

SACRED IN THE *Small*

SCRIPTURE

"Be still, and know that I am God."
– Psalm 46:10 (NIV)

DEVOTIONAL

Stillness feels impossible when you're being pulled in a hundred directions. But what if "being still" isn't about stopping everything, but simply acknowledging God in it all?

That moment when you rock a baby to sleep?
Sacred.
The coffee you sip before the chaos?
Sacred.
The whispered prayer while folding laundry?
Sacred.

Peace doesn't have to wait for a retreat or vacation. It can meet you in five minutes of stillness where you remember—God is here, and that's enough.

PRAYER

Lord, teach me to find stillness in the small spaces. Help me pause in the middle of my day and recognize You. Let Your presence bring peace to even the most ordinary moments. Amen.

REFLECTION

What are three small moments in your day where you can pause and become aware of God's presence?

_____

_____

_____

_____

_____

_____

_____

_____

_____

_____

THE INVITATION TO *Rest*

SCRIPTURE

"Come to me, all you who are weary and burdened, and I will give you rest." – Matthew 11:28 (NIV)

DEVOTIONAL

Rest isn't a reward—it's a holy invitation.

You don't have to earn it. You don't have to prove your worth first. Rest isn't something God holds out like a prize for those who finish the checklist or get motherhood "right." It's a gift, freely offered by the One who knows just how tired you really are.

Jesus isn't waiting for the calm, polished version of you. He sees you in the thick of it—in yoga pants and yesterday's mascara, with dishes piled up and voices raised in the next room. And that's the you He invites in. The one who's weary. The one who's burdened. The one who's trying her best and still wondering if it's enough.

His rest isn't an escape or a vacation. It's not found in a perfect nap or a silent house (though those are lovely when they happen). It's a soul-deep calm. A peace that enters right into the mess with you and reminds you: *You're not alone. You're held. You're loved.*

Let Him carry what's too heavy today. The worries about tomorrow. The guilt from yesterday. The impossible standards. He's big enough to hold it all—and gentle enough to carry you too.

PRAYER

Jesus, I bring You my tired body and anxious thoughts. Teach me to rest in Your presence, even in the middle of my busy life. Amen.

REFLECTION

What burden are you carrying that you need to place in Jesus' hands today?

_____

_____

_____

_____

_____

_____

_____

_____

THE *Peace* THAT GUARDS

SCRIPTURE

"The peace of God... will guard your hearts and your minds in Christ Jesus." – Philippians 4:7 (NIV)

DEVOTIONAL

Peace isn't the absence of noise or chaos— it's the steady presence of God right in the middle of it. We often imagine peace as a quiet home or a moment when everything finally falls into place. But true peace doesn't wait for calm circumstances; it anchors us even when life feels loud, messy, and unpredictable.

When anxiety rises, you don't need to fix everything before coming to God. He invites you to come as you are. His peace guards your heart and mind—not after the chaos ends, but in the middle of it. It's active, like a shield, surrounding you with comfort and strength.

Peace isn't a prize for getting life under control—it's a gift from the One who's already in control. You don't have to hold it all together. He's holding you. Let His presence settle your soul today.

PRAYER

Lord, guard my mind from anxious thoughts. Cover my heart in peace that doesn't make sense to the world. Let me walk today knowing I'm held by You. Amen.

REFLECTION

When your thoughts start to spiral, what truth from God's Word can you hold on to?

_____

_____

_____

_____

_____

_____

_____

_____

_____

_____

PURPOSE IN THE *Present*

SCRIPTURE

"This is the day the Lord has made; let us rejoice and be glad in it." – Psalm 118:24 (ESV)

DEVOTIONAL

It's easy to slip into "someday" thinking—believing that peace will come when the laundry is done, the schedule is lighter, or life finally feels manageable. But chasing a future version of rest can keep us from experiencing the presence of God right now. Peace isn't found in a perfect someday; it's found by stepping fully into today—exactly as it is. This moment, messy and beautiful, is where God wants to meet you.

God didn't accidentally give you this day. He crafted it with purpose, knowing both the struggles and the sweet spots it would hold. He's not waiting for a cleaner kitchen, calmer kids, or a quieter mind before He shows up. He's already here—in the noise, the chores, the small wins, and the hard moments. When you stop holding your breath for someday, you'll find the peace He's offering right here in the now.

PRAYER

Father, help me to be present today. Open my eyes to the sacred moments You've placed in this ordinary day. Amen.

REFLECTION

What's one small moment today where you saw God's hand at work?

_____

_____

_____

_____

_____

_____

_____

_____

_____

_____

_____

Grace FOR THE GAPS

SCRIPTURE

"My grace is sufficient for you, for my power is made perfect in weakness." – 2 Corinthians 12:9 (NIV)

DEVOTIONAL

Motherhood has a way of revealing every weakness—those moments when your patience wears thin, when you snap over small things, or when your energy is drained and you're barely holding it together. It's easy to see these as flaws, failures, or areas where you fall short. But what if they're not weaknesses to be fixed or hidden, but invitations from God? Invitations to rely on Him more fully, to acknowledge that you don't have it all together, and that's okay. He doesn't need you to be perfect; He longs for you to recognize your need for His grace.

God's grace was made for those very gaps— the moments when you're at the end of your rope, when you forget something important, or when you find yourself crying in the laundry room. His power doesn't wait until you have it all together. It shines brightest when your strength is gone, when you've reached your limit. In those moments, He steps in, fills the empty places, and offers a peace and strength that is not your own. Your weakness is where His grace can work most powerfully, reminding you that you are never alone, and His love covers every shortcoming.

PRAYER

Jesus, thank You for meeting me in my weakness. Let Your grace be enough for me today. Remind me that I don't have to be perfect—just present. Amen.

REFLECTION

Where have you been relying on your own strength? How can you lean into God's grace instead?

_____

_____

_____

_____

_____

_____

_____

_____

THE GIFT OF *Stillness*

SCRIPTURE

"Be still, and know that I am God."
– Psalm 46:10 (NIV)

DEVOTIONAL

Stillness isn't a luxury reserved for vacations or special moments—it's a lifeline in the everyday chaos. Even if it's just one minute of quiet while the kids nap or the car is still, that brief pause can make all the difference. It's in those moments of silence that you can reset your soul, take a deep breath, and find your footing again. Stillness isn't about escaping your responsibilities; it's about reconnecting with the peace that God offers, right in the middle of your busy life.

Peace begins when you choose to pause long enough to remember who God is—and that He's still in control. When life feels out of control, those small moments of stillness remind you that you don't have to carry it all on your own. God is sovereign, and His presence is always near. Even in the midst of the noise, He invites you to rest in His peace, knowing that He holds all things together.

PRAYER

God, in the middle of my noisy life, help me carve out stillness. Teach me to breathe deeply and trust fully. Amen.

REFLECTION

What small window of stillness can you build into your day?

_____

_____

_____

_____

_____

_____

_____

_____

_____

_____

_____

_____

_____

Surrendering CONTROL

SCRIPTURE

"Trust in the Lord with all your heart and lean not on your own understanding." – Proverbs 3:5 (NIV)

DEVOTIONAL

The desire to control every detail often stems from a place of fear—fear that things won't work out, fear that you're not enough, or fear of the unknown. It's easy to think that if we can manage every little piece of our lives, we'll somehow find security. But that sense of control is an illusion. Peace begins to grow when we loosen our grip and allow ourselves to trust in something greater than our own ability to manage it all. When we stop trying to control every outcome, we make room for God's peace to fill in the spaces.

God sees the whole picture, even when we can't. He knows the beginning, the middle, and the end, while we only see what's right in front of us. He invites us to trust Him with what we don't understand and to surrender the things we can't control. That kind of trust, in the midst of uncertainty, is where peace begins. It's in releasing the need to have all the answers that we find the calm we long for, knowing that God holds everything in His hands.

PRAYER

Lord, help me let go of the things I can't control. I trust You with my family, my future, and my today. Give me peace as I surrender it all to You. Amen.

REFLECTION

What's one thing you've been holding too tightly? What would surrender look like?

_____

_____

_____

_____

_____

_____

_____

_____

_____

Carried, NOT CRUSHED

SCRIPTURE

"We are hard pressed on every side, but not crushed… struck down, but not destroyed."
– 2 Corinthians 4:8-9 (NIV)

DEVOTIONAL

Motherhood brings pressure from all sides—expectations you put on yourself, comparisons to others, and the constant demands of caring for your family. It can feel overwhelming, like you're being stretched beyond your limit. But being hard-pressed doesn't mean you're broken beyond repair. It means you're human. And in that very place of strain, you are being held by a God who never lets go.

Even when the world feels like it's shaking, you are not alone, and you are not undone. God's strength surrounds you, even when yours is running low. His peace doesn't depend on how well you hold it all together—it rests on the truth that *He* is holding you. You can breathe deep knowing that the One who holds the universe also holds your heart, your home, and every hard moment.

PRAYER

Father, thank You for carrying me when life feels heavy. Let me feel Your strength today and remember that I am never alone. Amen.

REFLECTION

How has God carried you through a difficult season? How can that encourage you today?

_____

_____

_____

_____

_____

_____

_____

_____

_____

_____

WHO YOU *Are,* NOT WHAT YOU *Do*

SCRIPTURE

"See what great love the Father has lavished on us, that we should be called children of God!"
– 1 John 3:1 (NIV)

DEVOTIONAL

In a world that praises hustle and measures value by how much you get done, motherhood can start to feel like a never-ending performance. The to-do list never ends, and it's easy to believe your worth is tied to how well you manage it all. But God sees beyond what you accomplish. Your identity isn't built on clean floors, packed lunches, or crossed-off checklists—it's built on who you belong to.

You are more than the roles you fill. Before you were a mom, a wife, or a caretaker, you were—and still are—God's beloved daughter. That truth never changes, even when the dishes pile up or the day feels like a blur. When chaos swirls around you, let your soul rest in this: your value is secure, your name is known, and you are deeply loved by the One who calls you His own.

PRAYER

Lord, remind me today that I am Yours—loved, chosen, and held. Help me find peace not in what I do, but in who I am to You. Amen.

REFLECTION

What labels have you let define you lately? What would it look like to live out of your identity as God's child?

_____

_____

_____

_____

_____

_____

_____

_____

_____

_____

_____

THE *Patience* YOU DON'T HAVE

SCRIPTURE

"But the fruit of the Spirit is… patience."
– Galatians 5:22 (NIV)

DEVOTIONAL

Patience can feel miles away when your toddler is melting down in the grocery store or your teenager responds with silence and slammed doors. It's in those moments that your limits are tested and your emotions flare. But here's the good news—patience isn't something you have to muster up on your own. It's a fruit of the Spirit, something God cultivates in you as you stay close to Him. You're not failing because you feel frustrated—you're growing as you lean into His strength instead of your own.

Peace doesn't depend on your home being quiet or your kids behaving perfectly. It comes from being rooted in God, steady in Him even when everything around you feels unsteady. When you stay connected to the source—through prayer, Scripture, or simply pausing to breathe in His presence—you'll find He gives you what you need, moment by moment. Patience, peace, and strength are gifts He grows in you, right in the middle of real-life chaos.

PRAYER

Holy Spirit, grow patience in me today. Help me respond gently when I feel stretched thin. Remind me to pause and lean on You before I react. Amen.

REFLECTION

When was the last time you responded with grace instead of reaction? How can you make space to invite the Holy Spirit into your next challenging moment?

_____

_____

_____

_____

_____

_____

_____

_____

_____

Boundaries BRING PEACE

SCRIPTURE

"Let what you say be simply 'Yes' or 'No'; anything more comes from evil." – Matthew 5:37 (ESV)

DEVOTIONAL

Saying "yes" to everything leads to burnout—not blessing. Sometimes peace means saying "no" so you can say "yes" to the things that matter most. Jesus lived with holy boundaries. So can you. You're allowed to rest. You're allowed to protect your time. You're allowed to say "no" and still be loving.

Creating space in your life isn't neglect—it's nurture. When you stop overcommitting, you give yourself room to breathe, to listen for God's voice, and to focus on what truly matters. A busy life isn't always a faithful one. Peace often comes when you stop rushing and start resting in the rhythms of grace God designed for you.

PRAYER

God, give me the wisdom to know when to say no, and the courage to follow through. Help me create space for peace in my life by choosing what You want for me. Amen.

REFLECTION

What's one thing you've said "yes" to that might be stealing your peace? What would it look like to protect that space?

_____

_____

_____

_____

_____

_____

_____

_____

_____

_____

Peace IN THE MIDDLE OF WAITING

SCRIPTURE

"The Lord is good to those who wait for him, to the soul who seeks him." – Lamentations 3:25 (ESV)

DEVOTIONAL

Whether you're waiting on healing, breakthrough, or simply the end of a hard phase—waiting can feel like wilderness. But it's also where God meets you. He's not just at the finish line; He's in the quiet middle, shaping your heart and teaching you trust.

The waiting season isn't wasted—it's where roots grow deep. In the stillness, God is doing a work you may not see yet, strengthening your faith and preparing you for what's ahead. You don't have to rush through the waiting. You can rest in it, knowing He's already at work, and His timing is always right.

PRAYER

Lord, I don't like waiting, but I trust You in it. Help me believe that You are still good, even when things feel delayed or uncertain. Amen.

REFLECTION

What are you waiting on right now? How can you seek God in the middle of the wait instead of rushing past it?

_____

_____

_____

_____

_____

_____

_____

_____

_____

_____

_____

_____

_____

_____

_____

_____

Daily Bread, NOT A MONTHLY PLAN

SCRIPTURE

"Give us this day our daily bread."
– Matthew 6:11 (ESV)

DEVOTIONAL

You don't need to have a five-year plan to walk in peace. God promises to give you today's bread—strength for the moment, grace for this hour. Like manna in the desert, His provision is daily. You may feel like you're running on fumes, but God will keep showing up with enough.

You don't have to see the whole path to keep moving forward—you just need to trust the One who's leading. His faithfulness isn't reserved for future plans; it's present in your right-now needs. Peace comes not from having it all mapped out, but from knowing you're being guided by a God who never fails.

PRAYER

God, help me stop reaching for tomorrow's answers and instead trust You for today's strength. Remind me that You are my daily provider. Amen.

REFLECTION

What are you trying to plan or control right now? How might God be asking you to focus on today?

_____

_____

_____

_____

_____

_____

_____

_____

_____

_____

_____

YOU ARE *Not Alone*

SCRIPTURE

"Never will I leave you; never will I forsake you."
– Hebrews 13:5 (NIV)

DEVOTIONAL

Motherhood can feel isolating—especially when the tears and tantrums happen behind closed doors. But you're never parenting alone. God doesn't clock out. He's present in every diaper change, every school pickup, every bedtime story. His peace is rooted in His presence—and He never leaves.

Even when no one else sees the work you're doing, God does. He honors the unseen, uncelebrated moments with just as much care as the big ones. Every whispered prayer, every exhausted sigh, every act of love matters to Him. You're not invisible—you're deeply known and supported by the One who sees it all and walks with you through every part of it.

PRAYER

Father, thank You for being with me, even when I feel unseen. Help me to sense Your nearness today and let that truth quiet my heart. Amen.

REFLECTION

When was a time you felt God's presence in a lonely moment? How can you remember that closeness today?

_____

_____

_____

_____

_____

_____

_____

_____

_____

_____

HOLDING BOTH *Joy* AND *Chaos*

SCRIPTURE

"Rejoice in the Lord always; again I will say, rejoice."
– Philippians 4:4 (ESV)

DEVOTIONAL

Peace doesn't mean your problems disappear—it means you can experience deep joy even while walking through them. You can be tired and still laugh. You can feel stretched thin and still find moments of genuine delight. God's peace doesn't erase the hard parts; it steadies you in the middle of them, reminding you that joy and struggle can exist side by side.

When you choose to notice the beauty tucked inside the chaos—a quiet hug, a shared giggle, a small answered prayer—you're making space for peace to take root. It's not about waiting for calm to come; it's about letting God's presence meet you in the mess. That's where true peace grows—in the everyday moments you invite Him into.

PRAYER

Jesus, help me find joy today—not because everything is perfect, but because You are with me in it all. Let gratitude lead me to peace. Amen.

REFLECTION

What is one small thing that brought you joy today? How can you hold on to that moment and let it shape your perspective?

_____

_____

_____

_____

_____

_____

_____

_____

_____

_____

_____

_____

WHEN YOU FEEL *Invisible*

SCRIPTURE

"You are the God who sees me."
– Genesis 16:13 (NIV)

DEVOTIONAL

The lunches you pack, the laundry you fold, the late-night rocking and the early-morning chaos—so much of what you do is unseen. But not by God. He sees it all and He sees you. Your quiet sacrifices are not wasted. In the hidden places, He honors your faithfulness and meets you with peace.

Even when no one else notices or acknowledges the little things, God is present in them. Your acts of love, even the ones that seem ordinary or unnoticed, are precious to Him. The time and energy you pour into your family matter deeply, and He treasures every moment. His peace comes not only in the big, visible victories but in the small, quiet moments where you choose to serve with a heart full of love.

PRAYER

Lord, thank You for being the God who sees. Help me remember that even when no one else notices, You do. Let Your eyes on me be enough today. Amen.

REFLECTION

What hidden part of your motherhood feels unappreciated? How does it change things to know God sees it?

_____

_____

_____

_____

_____

_____

_____

_____

_____

_____

_____

Strength FOR TODAY

SCRIPTURE

"As your days, so shall your strength be."
– Deuteronomy 33:25 (ESV)

DEVOTIONAL

There are days when you wonder if you can keep going. But God promises not strength for the month—not even the week—just this day. That's how He carries you. One grace-soaked day at a time. Don't worry about tomorrow's energy. Just ask Him to help you with today's.

Each day, He gives you what you need for the moment you're in, whether it's patience, strength, or peace. It's easy to become overwhelmed when you look at everything ahead, but God's provision is always for the present. Trust that He will give you the grace you need for today, and tomorrow will have its own supply.

PRAYER

God, give me strength for this moment. When I feel worn down, remind me You are enough. Let me walk through today with Your peace and Your power. Amen.

REFLECTION

What part of today feels too heavy? Invite God into that space and ask Him for help—right now.

_____

_____

_____

_____

_____

_____

_____

_____

_____

_____

_____

_____

LETTING GO OF *Guilt*

SCRIPTURE

"There is now no condemnation for those who are in Christ Jesus." – Romans 8:1 (NIV)

DEVOTIONAL

Mom guilt is a master at whispering, You're not doing enough. You're messing them up. But God doesn't speak in guilt—He speaks in grace. He already knows your flaws and has covered them with His love. There's peace in knowing your failures don't disqualify you; they point you back to grace.

When guilt tries to pull you down, remember that God isn't surprised by your imperfections. He's not condemning you—He's inviting you into His arms of forgiveness and renewal. Each time you feel the weight of guilt, let it remind you to run to the One who offers unconditional grace. In His love, you find freedom, peace, and the strength to keep moving forward.

PRAYER

Jesus, free me from guilt that isn't from You. Help me to walk in Your forgiveness and parent from a place of grace. Amen.

REFLECTION

What's one lie guilt has been telling you? What truth from Scripture can you use to replace it?

_____

_____

_____

_____

_____

_____

_____

_____

_____

_____

_____

_____

PEACE IN *Transitions*

SCRIPTURE

"For everything there is a season..."
– Ecclesiastes 3:1 (ESV)

DEVOTIONAL

From newborns to teenagers, every phase brings new joys—and new chaos. Just when you think you've figured it out, something changes. But peace is possible in transition when you remember: God never changes. His love, strength, and promises are constant, even when life isn't.

Embrace the changes without fear, knowing that the One who holds your family's future also holds your heart in the present. The seasons of motherhood may shift, but God's faithfulness remains unwavering. His peace doesn't depend on stability—it depends on His unshakable presence, which is with you through every transition.

PRAYER

Father, as seasons shift, help me stay grounded in You. Let me hold each moment with open hands and trust You in the changes. Amen.

REFLECTION

What season are you in right now? How is God inviting you to trust Him through it?

_____

_____

_____

_____

_____

_____

_____

_____

_____

_____

_____

_____

CHOOSING *Peace* OVER *Perfection*

SCRIPTURE

"Martha, Martha... you are worried and upset about many things, but few things are needed—or indeed only one." – Luke 10:41-42 (NIV)

DEVOTIONAL

Martha wanted everything to be just right. Mary just wanted to be with Jesus. In your home, you get to choose: strive for perfection, or sit in peace. The dishes will wait. The laundry can pile. But your soul needs Jesus more than your house needs scrubbing.

Perfection isn't the goal—presence is. When you take a moment to pause and be with Him, you're choosing what truly matters. The chores will always be there, but those quiet moments with Jesus refresh and renew you in ways that nothing else can. Let your heart rest in His peace, knowing that He cares more for your connection with Him than for your to-do list.

PRAYER

Jesus, help me to choose presence over perfection.
Quiet my striving heart and teach me to rest with
You. Amen.

REFLECTION

What is one "Martha task" you can set aside today
to be more like Mary?

_____

_____

_____

_____

_____

_____

_____

_____

_____

_____

_____

_____

HIS WORD *Anchors* YOU

SCRIPTURE

"Your word is a lamp to my feet and a light to my path." – Psalm 119:105 (ESV)

DEVOTIONAL

When life feels dark, overwhelming, or uncertain, it's easy to want a full roadmap—clear answers, guaranteed outcomes, and a sense of control. But God rarely gives the full picture. Instead, He offers light for the next step, not the entire path. His Word becomes a lamp to your feet (Psalm 119:105), gently guiding you forward, one decision, one breath, one prayer at a time. In seasons of confusion, it's not more clarity we need first—it's more of Him. And His presence is often found right there, waiting in the pages of Scripture.

You don't need an hour-long quiet time or the perfect setting to hear from God. Just opening your Bible—even for five minutes in the middle of a messy day—can shift your perspective, calm your spirit, and realign your heart with His. That moment of connection becomes an anchor in the chaos. The world may still swirl, but inside, peace begins to return. God's Word doesn't just inform—it transforms, lighting the way and reminding you that you're not walking through the dark alone.

PRAYER

God, let Your Word guide me today. Speak to me through Scripture and anchor my heart in Your truth. Amen.

REFLECTION

What Scripture has brought you peace in the past? Can you return to it this week?

_____

_____

_____

_____

_____

_____

_____

_____

_____

_____

YOUR PEACE IS A *Gift* TO YOUR FAMILY

SCRIPTURE

"Let the peace of Christ rule in your hearts... and be thankful." – Colossians 3:15 (NIV)

DEVOTIONAL

When you choose peace, it doesn't just affect your heart—it changes the atmosphere around you. Your calm becomes a covering for your home, a place where your children can exhale and your family can feel safe. Peace doesn't mean you never raise your voice or have hard days. It means you're anchored. It means that even when things unravel, there's a steady presence in the storm—because you've made space for God's presence first. Your decision to seek peace, even in small moments, becomes a gift to everyone who lives under your roof.

A peaceful mom isn't a perfect one. She's the one who knows where to run when things fall apart. She comes back to Jesus again and again—not out of guilt, but because she's learning that grace is her rhythm and dependence is her strength. That kind of faith becomes a refuge for your children.

They learn, not from your perfection, but from your posture—how you turn toward God when things get hard. And in that, they learn where to find peace for themselves, too.

PRAYER

Jesus, let Your peace rule in my heart so it can flow into my home. Use me to bring calm into my family today. Amen.

REFLECTION

How does your peace (or lack of it) impact the atmosphere in your home? What might shift if you prioritized your own inner stillness with God?

Peace WHEN YOU'RE OVERSTIMULATED

SCRIPTURE

"He leads me beside quiet waters. He refreshes my soul." – Psalm 23:2-3 (NIV)

DEVOTIONAL

The noise never seems to stop—crying from the baby monitor, constant questions from curious little minds, the hum of devices, and the never-ending stream of demands on your time and attention. As a mom, you're constantly pouring out, responding, and managing a dozen things at once. But you weren't created to absorb it all without pause. Even Jesus stepped away from the crowds to rest and pray. He knows your limits and doesn't expect you to be superhuman. In fact, He lovingly reminds you that rest isn't weakness—it's wisdom.

In the middle of the chaos, Jesus invites you to find a pocket of quiet—not an hour of solitude, but a sacred pause. Maybe it's five minutes behind a locked bathroom door, a deep breath before you walk into the next room, or a whispered prayer while stirring dinner. He doesn't need silence to speak; He just needs your heart turned toward Him. And when you do, He meets you there—offering strength, gentleness, and the peace your soul is craving. Even small moments with Him can refill what's been emptied.

PRAYER

Good Shepherd, lead me to quiet waters today. Refresh me when my senses feel overloaded. Let Your peace wash over the noise. Amen.

REFLECTION

Where can you build in a short "quiet waters" moment today?

_____

_____

_____

_____

_____

_____

_____

_____

LETTING GO OF *Control*

SCRIPTURE

"Trust in the Lord with all your heart and lean not on your own understanding." – Proverbs 3:5 (NIV)

DEVOTIONAL

As a mom, it's easy to feel the weight of everything—how your kids turn out, how smoothly the day goes, how your own body reacts to exhaustion or anxiety. The desire to hold it all together can feel overwhelming. But the truth is, you were never meant to control it all. Control is a burden that belongs to God, not you. He sees the bigger picture, knows the hearts of your children, and holds tomorrow in His hands. When you try to manage outcomes that only He can shape, you carry a weight you were never designed to bear.

God isn't asking you to fix every problem or predict every outcome—He's inviting you to trust Him. Peace doesn't come when everything finally lines up the way you hoped. It comes when you open your hands, release your grip, and rest in the fact that He is faithful. Surrender isn't giving up; it's giving over—to the One who's far more capable than you. The moment you let go of what was never yours to manage is the moment peace starts to take root, deep in your soul.

PRAYER

Lord, help me loosen my grip on what I cannot control. I trust Your heart, even when I don't understand Your hand. Amen.

REFLECTION

What's one thing you need to surrender today? Say it out loud and offer it to God.

_____

_____

_____

_____

_____

_____

_____

_____

_____

_____

_____

PEACE IN THE MIDDLE OF

SCRIPTURE

"Blessed are the peacemakers, for they will be called children of God." – Matthew 5:9 (NIV)

DEVOTIONAL

When voices rise and tempers flare—between siblings, spouses, or even within your own heart— you often find yourself in the middle. As a mom, you're the peacemaker, the referee, the one trying to bring calm into the chaos. It can feel exhausting and thankless, but what you're doing matters deeply. You're not just breaking up arguments or diffusing tension; you're shaping hearts and creating a culture of grace. Each time you breathe deeply instead of snapping, each time you step in with wisdom instead of weariness, you're teaching your children what it looks like to seek peace.

Your quiet strength plants seeds that may not bloom right away but will grow over time. When you choose to forgive out loud, speak kindly in hard moments, or admit your own mistakes with humility, you're modeling the very heart of God. Peace doesn't always look like perfection—it looks like presence, patience, and perseverance. And in those hard, holy moments of motherhood, you are reflecting God's character in a way that your children will carry with them long after the moment has passed.

PRAYER

Father, make me a peacemaker in my home. Help me speak life when conflict rises and teach my children to follow You in love. Amen.

REFLECTION

How can you model peace today in the way you respond to sibling chaos?

_____

_____

_____

_____

_____

_____

_____

_____

_____

_____

PEACE WHEN YOU'RE *Disappointed*

SCRIPTURE

"The Lord is close to the brokenhearted and saves those who are crushed in spirit." – Psalm 34:18 (NIV)

DEVOTIONAL

Sometimes motherhood brings a quiet kind of heartbreak—disappointments you didn't see coming, expectations that went unmet, relationships that feel strained, or dreams that seem to be on indefinite hold. It's the ache of giving your all and still feeling like it wasn't enough. In those moments, it's easy to wonder if God sees you, if He cares about the silent tears and hidden frustrations. But the truth is, He's never been closer. God doesn't shy away from your sadness; He draws near to the brokenhearted and gently gathers your pain into His hands.

Peace in these seasons doesn't come from pretending everything's okay. It comes from knowing you're not alone in your sorrow. God sits with you in the dark places—not rushing you through them, but holding you through them. He is the God who promises beauty from ashes, hope in waiting, and purpose even in pain. When you invite Him into your disappointment, He begins the quiet work of healing—transforming what feels like loss into something sacred and deeply good in His time.

PRAYER

Jesus, hold my heart in this disappointment. Be close and help me believe You're still working even in the sorrow. Amen.

REFLECTION

What loss or unmet hope are you grieving? Invite God into that space with you.

_____

_____

_____

_____

_____

_____

_____

_____

_____

WHEN YOU'VE LOST YOUR *Temper*

SCRIPTURE

"The Lord is compassionate and gracious, slow to anger, abounding in love." – Psalm 103:8 (NIV)

DEVOTIONAL

You didn't mean to lose your temper—but it happened. The words came out too fast, too sharp, and now the guilt is heavy. Maybe it wasn't the first time this week. Maybe you're starting to wonder if you'll ever get it right. But here's the truth: God's mercy isn't based on your performance. He's not tallying your failures or waiting for you to earn your way back to grace. He sees the heaviness in your heart, and instead of turning away, He leans in with compassion. He doesn't cancel you; He gently corrects and restores you in love.

There is always room to reset. You can take a breath, offer a genuine apology, and try again. That simple act of humility models something powerful for your children—what it looks like to live in grace, not perfection. God's peace doesn't depend on flawless behavior; it flows from His unchanging presence. Even after the yelling, even in the mess, He offers a fresh start. His grace is what makes peace possible—not just in your home, but in your heart.

PRAYER

God, thank You for Your mercy when I mess up. Help me apologize well and try again with gentleness. Teach me to reflect Your love. Amen.

REFLECTION

What does it look like to receive grace and start fresh today?

_____

_____

_____

_____

_____

_____

_____

_____

_____

_____

_____

WHEN YOU FEEL *Behind*

SCRIPTURE

"There is a time for everything, and a season for
every activity under the heavens."
– Ecclesiastes 3:1 (NIV)

DEVOTIONAL

The dishes are still in the sink, the laundry is
growing into a mountain, and your to-do list looks
exactly the same as it did this morning. You feel like
you're behind before the day even ends, like you
just can't catch up. It's easy to equate productivity
with purpose and to believe the lie that you're failing
when things go unfinished. But God isn't looking at
your checklist—He's looking at your heart. What
if, in His eyes, you're not behind at all? What if He's
more concerned with your faithfulness than your
efficiency?

God doesn't measure your worth by how
much you accomplish. He's not rushed, and He's
not asking you to live at a frantic pace. Sometimes
peace comes not from doing more, but from
choosing to slow down and trust that His timing
is better than your own. When you release the

pressure to perform and lean into His pace, you'll begin to see that even the slow, ordinary moments have sacred purpose. You're not late. You're not lost. You're right where He's leading you—one grace-filled step at a time.

PRAYER

Lord, help me release the lie that I must always catch up. Let me rest in the rhythm of grace You've set for me. Amen.

REFLECTION

What are you pressuring yourself to finish? Ask God if it truly matters today.

_____

_____

_____

_____

_____

_____

_____

_____

_____

_____

THE GIFT OF *Small* FAITHFULNESS

SCRIPTURE

"Whoever can be trusted with very little can also be trusted with much." – Luke 16:10 (NIV)

DEVOTIONAL

Wiping noses, packing lunches, folding the same pile of laundry for the hundredth time—it can start to feel like your days are made up of invisible tasks that no one notices or appreciates. The repetition can wear on your heart, and you might wonder if any of it really matters. But in God's eyes, faithfulness in the small things is deeply significant. Every quiet act of love, every unseen sacrifice, every ordinary moment offered with a willing heart is seen and valued by Him. You're not just doing chores—you're building something sacred.

God has a way of turning the smallest seeds into something eternal. When you choose to love through service, to show up even when you're tired, or to keep going when it feels thankless, you're laying a foundation of peace that your family can stand on. These moments, though seemingly simple, become holy ground. They teach your children what love looks like in action and create a home where grace can grow. In God's hands, your everyday faithfulness becomes something far greater than you can see right now.

PRAYER

Father, help me stay faithful in the small things. Remind me that nothing done in love is ever wasted in Your kingdom. Amen.

REFLECTION

What small act of love can you offer today as a gift to God?

_____

_____

_____

_____

_____

_____

_____

_____

_____

WHEN THE FUTURE FEELS *Scary*

SCRIPTURE

"Therefore do not worry about tomorrow, for
tomorrow will worry about itself."
– Matthew 6:34 (NIV)

DEVOTIONAL

What if they don't make good choices? What
if the money runs out? What if something happens
to someone you love? The "what ifs" of motherhood
can be relentless, pulling your thoughts into a
whirlwind of fear and uncertainty. It's natural to want
to protect, prepare, and plan for every possible
outcome. But the truth is, no amount of worrying
can secure the future. That kind of weight was never
meant for your shoulders. The good news? God
is already there. He's not just present in today's
mess—He's sovereign over what's coming next.

Peace begins when you stop trying to control
the unknown and start entrusting it to the One who
already knows. God holds tomorrow, just as surely
as He's holding you today. Each time you choose to
trust Him with what hasn't happened yet, you plant
a seed of peace in your heart. Trust doesn't silence

every fear, but it shifts your focus—from the storm of "what ifs" to the steady presence of the One who never changes. He is faithful. And that truth is what gives you the courage to breathe deep and move forward, one grace-filled step at a time.

PRAYER

God, I release the fear of what might come. Help me live in today, knowing You are already in my tomorrow. Amen.

REFLECTION

Write down your biggest fears about the future—and then write "God is bigger" beside it.

_____

_____

_____

_____

_____

_____

_____

_____

_____

PEACE IN THE *Routine*

SCRIPTURE

"So whether you eat or drink or whatever you do, do it all for the glory of God." – 1 Corinthians 10:31 (NIV)

DEVOTIONAL

Life as a mom often feels like a never-ending cycle of repetition—diapers, dishes, discipline, and then repeat. The days can blur together, filled with tasks that seem small or insignificant in the grand scheme of things. It's easy to feel like your work is unnoticed or unimportant. But God isn't bored by your routine; He's present in every moment of it. He doesn't see your days as monotonous—He sees them as opportunities for love and service. Every diaper change, every meal prepared, every load of laundry folded is infused with purpose when done with a heart of love.

There's a profound peace that comes from realizing your everyday work is sacred. The sacredness doesn't come from the task itself, but from the heart behind it. When you offer your mundane moments to God—when you choose to serve with grace and joy, even in the smallest acts—

you are worshiping Him. That's where the peace lies: knowing that your routine is meaningful to Him, that He sees you, and that you're reflecting His love in everything you do. Even the simplest acts, when done with a heart devoted to Him, become an offering of worship.

PRAYER

Lord, meet me in the everyday. Help me glorify You through the small, repeated acts of love. Amen.

REFLECTION

How can you view one repetitive task today as worship?

_____

_____

_____

_____

_____

_____

_____

_____

_____

WHEN YOU'RE *Waiting* ON A BREAKTHROUGH

SCRIPTURE

"Wait for the Lord; be strong and take heart and wait for the Lord." – Psalm 27:14 (NIV)

DEVOTIONAL

Maybe you're waiting for healing, help, or even just a good night's sleep. The wait can feel long, frustrating, and far from peaceful. It's easy to see waiting as a place of inactivity or stagnation, but in reality, it's often where God does His deepest work. Waiting doesn't mean God is absent—it means He's at work beneath the surface, even when you can't see it. It's in these quiet, often uncomfortable moments that He's shaping your character, refining your faith, and drawing you closer to Him.

You may not see the results of your waiting yet, but that doesn't mean nothing is happening. Like a tree whose roots grow deep before the fruit appears, God is establishing strength and resilience in you, even in the unseen moments. Trust that He is moving, even when the answers haven't come. Peace comes not from rushing through the wait, but from trusting that God is growing something in you during this time. You don't have to have it all figured out—just keep trusting, and in due time, the fruit will come.

PRAYER

Jesus, give me the strength to wait with hope. Let my trust grow deeper while I wait for what I cannot yet see. Amen.

REFLECTION

What are you waiting for right now? What truth can help anchor you in the meantime?

_____

_____

_____

_____

_____

_____

_____

_____

_____

YOU ARE *Not* ALONE

SCRIPTURE

"Never will I leave you; never will I forsake you."
– Hebrews 13:5 (NIV)

DEVOTIONAL

Some days, it feels like the weight of your entire family rests on your shoulders. You carry the responsibility of managing the household, meeting everyone's needs, and keeping things running smoothly. The tasks seem endless, and in those moments, it's easy to feel isolated, as though you're the only one holding it all together. But here's the truth: You are never alone in this. Even in the most mundane moments, God is right there with you. He is walking with you through the grocery aisles, offering patience as you navigate tantrums, and providing strength through the late-night feedings. No part of your day is outside of His care.

His presence is the peace you need, especially when it feels like everything is falling on you. You don't have to carry the weight alone because He is carrying it with you, and often, He's carrying more of it than you realize. When you turn to Him, even in the chaos, you invite His peace to settle over your heart. That peace doesn't remove the struggles, but it gives you a deep sense of calm and assurance, knowing that He's with you, and that He sees every sacrifice, every tear, and every effort you make.

PRAYER

Father, thank You for never leaving me. Help me feel Your presence today and know I am not walking alone. Amen.

REFLECTION

Where do you feel the loneliest in motherhood? Invite God into that space.

_____

_____

_____

_____

_____

_____

_____

_____

_____

PEACE IN YOUR *Body*

SCRIPTURE

"Do you not know that your bodies are temples of the Holy Spirit...?" – 1 Corinthians 6:19 (NIV)

DEVOTIONAL

Your body carries so much: the weight of children in your arms, the groceries from the store, the stress of daily demands, and the exhaustion from sleepless nights. It can start to feel like you're running on empty, and it's easy to be discouraged when you look in the mirror and see the physical toll that life is taking. The aches, the tired eyes, the changes in your appearance—they can all become a reminder of how much you've given, how much you're holding. But in the midst of that, remember this truth: God calls your body holy. He doesn't see it as a burden or something to be ashamed of. He sees it as His sacred dwelling place.

God doesn't shame your body for its weariness or imperfections. Instead, He honors it—because it's the vessel He's chosen to carry His Spirit. When you choose to speak peace to your body, you remind yourself of the truth that God sees you as beautiful and strong, just as you are. Your body, though fragile, is deeply loved by the Creator. It is capable of amazing things, even in its tiredness. Speak to your body today with words of peace, gratitude, and care. Your worth isn't determined by how you look or feel, but by the love God has for you, the love He has infused into every part of you.

PRAYER

God, thank You for this body that serves my family so well. Help me see it the way You do—with gratitude and kindness. Amen.

REFLECTION

What can you do today to treat your body with gentleness and honor?

_____

_____

_____

_____

_____

_____

_____

_____

SCRIPTURE

"But he said to me, 'My grace is sufficient for you, for my power is made perfect in weakness.'"
– 2 Corinthians 12:9 (NIV)

DEVOTIONAL

Parenting often feels like a never-ending journey of mistakes—saying the wrong thing in the heat of the moment, forgetting a school project, or losing your patience when you promised yourself you wouldn't. It's easy to become consumed by guilt, feeling like you're failing your children or falling short of the parent you want to be. In those moments, it can be hard to see past your imperfections. But the truth is, God doesn't expect you to be perfect. Parenting isn't about flawless performance; it's about leaning into His grace in the midst of your shortcomings. Your mistakes don't disqualify you from being a good mom—they make you human.

God's grace is big enough to fill in the gaps. He's not asking for you to get it right every time— He's asking for you to surrender to Him in your weaknesses. It's in those moments of imperfection that His power is most evident. When you come before Him with humility, acknowledging your need for His help, He meets you with love and grace. His grace doesn't just cover your mistakes—it transforms them. Your weakness doesn't disqualify you; it positions you perfectly for God to show up in a way that displays His strength. And in the process, you're teaching your children the beauty of grace, forgiveness, and the freedom that comes from trusting God with your imperfections.

PRAYER

Jesus, I bring You my parenting failures. Thank You for Your grace. Help me parent from a place of humility and peace. Amen.

REFLECTION

What recent mistake are you holding onto? Give it to Jesus—and let it go.

_____

_____

_____

_____

_____

_____

Joy RESTORES *Peace*

SCRIPTURE

"The joy of the Lord is your strength."
– Nehemiah 8:10 (NIV)

DEVOTIONAL

Peace and joy are inseparable—they go hand in hand, like sisters who run together through the ups and downs of life. When joy begins to fade, it's often a sign that peace is slipping away too. Life's stresses and struggles can steal both joy and peace, leaving you feeling overwhelmed or burdened. But here's the good news: you don't have to wait for everything to be perfect to find joy. Sometimes, the most refreshing way to reset your spirit is through simple, intentional acts that invite joy back in. Whether it's laughing with your kids, playing your favorite worship song, or stepping outside for a few moments of fresh air, these small moments can reignite the joy that sustains your peace.

Joy doesn't ignore the hard moments of life—it simply refuses to stay stuck in them. It acknowledges the challenges but chooses to look beyond them, finding reasons to celebrate even in the midst of hardship. When you choose joy, even on the tough days, it creates a space for peace to take root. It's not about pretending everything is fine, but about choosing to find moments of light and gratitude in the midst of the mess. Peace and joy work together to remind you that, no matter how difficult things may feel, God is still good, and His joy is always available to you.

PRAYER

Lord, restore my joy today. Let it be the strength that carries me forward and the spark that revives my peace. Amen.

REFLECTION

What brings you joy? Choose one joyful thing to do today—on purpose.

_____

_____

_____

_____

_____

_____

_____

_____

WHEN YOU *feel* UNSEEN

SCRIPTURE

"You are the God who sees me."
– Genesis 16:13 (NIV)

DEVOTIONAL

As a mom, so much of your work happens behind the scenes—picking up toys, wiping away tears, preparing meals, and praying over your children while they sleep. These acts often go unnoticed by others, and it's easy to feel invisible, as if no one sees or appreciates the countless ways you give of yourself every day. The world may overlook the quiet sacrifices, the late nights, and the moments where you put your own needs aside for the sake of your family. But here's the truth: God sees it all. He notices every small, unseen act of love. Every time you choose to serve with grace, every sacrifice made in the quiet corners of your home, is seen by the One who cherishes you.

God doesn't miss a thing. He honors what others might overlook or take for granted. While the world may not always recognize your efforts, He does. You are never invisible to Him. In fact, He delights in your heart of service, your dedication, and your love for your family. Even in the quiet moments when no one else is around to say thank you, God is with you, and He is proud of you. You are His beloved daughter, and every act of love and care you give is an offering to Him. You are never unnoticed by Him; He treasures your faithfulness and rewards the quiet labor of your love.

PRAYER

God who sees, thank You for noticing the little things. Help me remember that my faithfulness matters to You, even when no one else claps. Amen.

REFLECTION

What is one unnoticed task you do every day? Offer it to God as worship today.

PEACE IN *Transitions*

SCRIPTURE

"Jesus Christ is the same yesterday and today and forever." – Hebrews 13:8 (NIV)

DEVOTIONAL

Kids grow so quickly, schedules shift, and seasons of life come and go. Each transition—whether it's a child moving into a new grade, a change in routine, or a shift in family dynamics—can feel like a balancing act. These changes stretch us, often leaving us feeling off-balance and uncertain. The familiar routines we once clung to begin to fade, and it's easy to feel like we're losing our footing. But even in the midst of transition, there's one unchanging truth: Jesus remains constant. While everything around us may be in flux, He is the steady anchor that holds us in place. His presence doesn't shift with the seasons—He is the same yesterday, today, and forever.

As you walk through each new phase of life, remember that you are never alone in the process. Jesus doesn't just stand by while you face these changes—He walks with you, guiding you through every transition. He understands the difficulty of stepping into something new, and He promises to be your strength when you feel weak, your peace when you feel anxious, and your anchor when everything else feels unsteady. With Him by your side, you can face the challenges of change with confidence, knowing that He will remain constant and faithful, no matter what season you're in.

PRAYER

Jesus, You never change. Be my steady place as everything around me shifts. Hold me close when I feel unsteady. Amen.

REFLECTION

What transition are you walking through right now? How can you invite God into it?

_____

_____

_____

_____

_____

_____

_____

_____

WHEN YOU'RE RUNNING ON *Empty*

SCRIPTURE

"Come to me, all you who are weary and burdened, and I will give you rest." – Matthew 11:28 (NIV)

DEVOTIONAL

There are days when it feels like you've given everything—your time, your energy, your love, and your care. You pour into your family, serve others, and meet every need, only to find that by the end of the day, there's nothing left for yourself. You collapse into bed, physically drained, mentally exhausted, and emotionally spent. In those moments, it's easy to feel like you have to keep pushing, to power through the exhaustion and do it all over again tomorrow. But Jesus doesn't ask you to power through. He knows the weight of your load, and He doesn't want you to carry it alone. Instead, He invites you to come to Him, to rest in His presence, and to allow His peace to replenish you.

When you rest in Him, He restores what burnout drains. His presence isn't just a momentary break—it's a deep, soul-refreshing rest that renews your strength. Jesus offers you more than temporary relief; He offers lasting restoration. It's in His presence that you find the peace and energy you need to face another day, not because you've simply had a break, but because He's filled you up with His love and grace. When you rest in Him, you allow His power to work in you, replenishing your heart and spirit so that you can keep serving with joy and love, knowing that He is always there to strengthen and sustain you.

PRAYER

Lord, I'm tired. Fill the empty places with Your presence and remind me that it's okay to slow down. Amen.

REFLECTION

What's one thing you can say no to this week in order to find rest?

_____

_____

_____

_____

_____

_____

_____

WHEN YOU'RE COMPARING *Yourself*

SCRIPTURE

"Each of you should test your own actions. Then you can take pride in yourself, without comparing yourself to someone else." – Galatians 6:4 (NIV)

DEVOTIONAL

It's easy to look at others and feel like you're falling short—her house is always spotless, her kids seem well-behaved, and her social media is full of picture-perfect moments. Comparison has a way of stealing peace, making you forget the beautiful things God is doing in your own life. What you see on the outside doesn't tell the full story. You're only seeing a snapshot of someone's journey, and it's often not the whole picture. When you compare yourself to others, you miss the unique way God is working in your life.

Remember, you were never called to be someone else. You were chosen to be you, with all your strengths, weaknesses, and beautiful, messy moments. God's plan for you is unique, and you're doing better than you think. The peace you long for comes from embracing who He made you to be, not trying to measure up to someone else's life. Trust that He is at work in you, and you are exactly where you need to be.

PRAYER

God, protect me from the trap of comparison. Help me see my life through Your eyes—not through someone else's highlight reel. Amen.

REFLECTION

Who or what do you often compare yourself to? Ask God to help you release that pressure.

_____

_____

_____

_____

_____

_____

_____

_____

_____

_____

_____

SCRIPTURE

"He gently leads those that have young."
– Isaiah 40:11 (NIV)

DEVOTIONAL

There are days when you feel like you've failed as a mom—maybe you yelled when you didn't want to, forgot an important permission slip, or handed over the screen too quickly in moments of exhaustion. The guilt creeps in, and it's easy to fear that you're somehow ruining your kids. But in those moments, remember that God isn't shouting at you in condemnation—He's gently leading you with grace. He understands your humanity, and He isn't expecting perfection. Instead, He meets you with love, compassion, and a call to grow.

God's grace covers your gaps, filling in the places where you fall short. His Spirit is right there, teaching you day by day, helping you become the mom He has called you to be. Each day is an opportunity to learn, to apologize when needed, and to grow in grace. You're not ruining your kids; you're learning alongside them. With God's guidance, you'll find strength, wisdom, and patience, even in the most challenging moments.

PRAYER

Jesus, when I feel like I'm failing, remind me that You are leading. Thank You for loving me gently as I learn and grow. Amen.

REFLECTION

Where do you feel like you're failing? How can you offer that fear to God today?

_____

_____

_____

_____

_____

_____

_____

_____

_____

_____

_____

PEACE THROUGH *Gratitude*

SCRIPTURE

"Give thanks in all circumstances; for this is God's will for you in Christ Jesus."
– 1 Thessalonians 5:18 (NIV)

DEVOTIONAL

Gratitude is a powerful doorway to peace. It doesn't remove the chaos or make life perfect, but it shifts your perspective. Instead of focusing on everything that's going wrong, gratitude allows you to reframe your circumstances, even if just for a moment. When you thank God for small blessings—a baby's sweet giggle, the warmth of a hot meal, or a fleeting moment of quiet—it helps you find peace right where you are. In the midst of all the noise, gratitude centers your heart on the goodness that God is still showing you, even in the mess.

When you choose gratitude, your heart begins to settle. It becomes easier to see the blessings that surround you, and as you focus on God's goodness, you're reminded that He is always at work, even in the smallest moments. Gratitude grounds you in the truth that God is good, that He is present, and that

He is faithful. No matter what chaos may be swirling around, gratitude helps you hold onto peace and stay anchored in His love.

PRAYER

Lord, help me see Your goodness all around me. Give me a thankful heart that welcomes peace. Amen.

REFLECTION

Write down 3 things you're thankful for today—big or small.

_____

_____

_____

_____

_____

_____

_____

_____

_____

_____

_____

CHOOSING PEACE OVER *Perfection*

SCRIPTURE

"Give thanks in all circumstances; for this is God's will for you in Christ Jesus."
– 1 Thessalonians 5:18 (NIV)

DEVOTIONAL

Martha's desire to make everything perfect led her to become overwhelmed by the details of preparing a meal and making her home just right. She wanted to give Jesus her best, but in the process, she missed the opportunity to simply be with Him. Jesus gently reminded her that He wasn't asking for perfection—He was asking for her presence. Just like Martha, we often find ourselves running around, trying to make everything perfect for our families, but peace doesn't come from getting it all right. It comes from choosing to pause and rest in God's presence, even when the to-do list seems endless.

As a mom, you don't have to be the perfect mom with the perfect house. Peace isn't found in flawless performance—it's found in choosing what is better: sitting at Jesus' feet, surrendering your worries, and trusting that He is enough. When you stop striving for perfection and choose His presence over perfection, your heart will find rest. Peace comes when you allow yourself the grace to be present in the moment, even if the laundry isn't folded and the dishes aren't done. Jesus values your heart, not your performance.

PRAYER

Jesus, I choose You over my to-do list. Help me let go of perfection and lean into what matters most. Amen.

REFLECTION

Where are you striving for perfection? What would it look like to choose peace instead?

_____

_____

_____

_____

_____

_____

_____

_____

BE REMINDED WHO YOU *Are*

SCRIPTURE

"You are God's masterpiece, created in Christ Jesus to do good works." – Ephesians 2:10 (NLT)

DEVOTIONAL

It's easy to get caught up in the daily grind of motherhood—changing diapers, making snacks, keeping track of schedules, and feeling like you're just going through the motions. On those days when you look in the mirror and see tired eyes or feel like you're not doing enough, it can be easy to forget your worth. But you are more than just the tasks you perform. You are God's masterpiece, intricately designed and deeply loved by Him. Your value isn't found in your ability to check off to-do lists or keep everything running smoothly; your worth is found in the fact that you were created by God, with purpose and intention.

Even on the hard days when you feel small or insignificant, remember that your identity is rooted in Christ, not your productivity. You were created for a unique purpose, and no amount of exhaustion or uncompleted tasks can take that away. When you rest in the truth of who God made you to be, you can find peace in knowing that He sees you, He loves you, and you are enough in His eyes. Your role as a mom is important, but it does not define you. You are a beloved daughter of God, and that is where your true identity lies.

PRAYER

Lord, remind me today that I am Your beloved. Let that truth settle deeper than any failure or insecurity. Amen.

REFLECTION

How do you define yourself lately—and how might God define you differently?

_____

_____

_____

_____

_____

_____

_____

_____

_____

WHEN YOU'RE *Craving* CONNECTION

SCRIPTURE

"Carry each other's burdens, and in this way you will fulfill the law of Christ." – Galatians 6:2 (NIV)

DEVOTIONAL

Motherhood can be incredibly isolating, even when you're surrounded by people. You might be holding a baby in one arm, stirring dinner with the other, and still feel completely unseen. The truth is, you were never meant to do this alone. You need others—people who understand the chaos, who won't flinch at your mess, who can remind you of grace when you're too tired to remember it yourself. You need friends who will pray when you forget how and listen when words don't come easily. Real community doesn't require perfection—it invites honesty.

There is deep peace in being known and supported. God designed us for connection, and leaning on others is not a sign of weakness—it's a step toward wholeness. Don't let pride or fear keep you from reaching out. Whether it's a text, a coffee meet-up, or simply admitting that you're struggling, opening that door can bring unexpected relief. You're not meant to carry life alone—and you don't have to. Let others in, and let peace grow in the space where grace and friendship meet.

PRAYER

God, bring me the right people—friends who see me, support me, and help me grow in You. Help me be that friend for others too. Amen.

REFLECTION

Is there someone you could open up to this week— or someone who may need you to reach out?

_____

_____

_____

_____

_____

_____

_____

_____

_____

_____

PEACE IN *Discipline*

SCRIPTURE

"No discipline seems pleasant at the time, but painful. Later on, however, it produces a harvest of righteousness and peace." – Hebrews 12:11 (NIV)

DEVOTIONAL

Correcting your child can be one of the most draining parts of motherhood. You repeat yourself, set boundaries, and wonder if anything is sinking in. It's tempting to feel discouraged, especially when the results aren't immediate. But discipline, when done in love, is a gift—not just to your child, but to your home. It teaches security, respect, and wisdom. Even when it's hard, these moments are sacred investments. You're not just managing behavior—you're shaping character, planting seeds that will grow in time.

God models this with us. He disciplines His children not out of frustration or punishment, but out of deep, steady love. He's patient, kind, and intentional—and He invites you to reflect that same grace-filled approach. So when you enter those hard conversations, do it with peace. You're not alone in it. God is working through your effort, shaping hearts (yours included), and growing something lasting, even if it doesn't look like progress right away.

PRAYER

Father, help me discipline with love, not frustration. Give me wisdom, patience, and long-term vision. Amen.

REFLECTION

What's one way you can bring peace into the way you discipline today?

_____

_____

_____

_____

_____

_____

_____

_____

_____

WHEN YOU'RE *Spiritually Dry*

SCRIPTURE

"Blessed are those who hunger and thirst for righteousness, for they will be filled."
– Matthew 5:6 (NIV)

DEVOTIONAL

Sometimes your soul feels quiet in a way that isn't peaceful—just tired. You don't feel like praying. Your Bible collects dust while your mind spins with a thousand other things. You wonder if you're drifting, if God notices, or if He's disappointed. But God doesn't shame you for feeling dry or distant. He doesn't withdraw in frustration. Instead, He gently invites you back, not with demands, but with grace. Even the faintest whisper—"God, I miss You"—is enough to open the door.

The beautiful truth is that He meets you where you are, not where you think you should be. You don't have to come with a perfectly prepared heart—just a willing one. When you seek Him, even imperfectly, He promises to draw near and to fill your emptiness with His presence. Spiritual dryness isn't the end; it can be the beginning of deeper dependence. Let your hunger lead you to the One who satisfies.

PRAYER

Lord, I feel dry and distant. Meet me here. Refresh my soul and awaken a hunger for You again. Amen.

REFLECTION

What is one small way you can reconnect with God today?

_____

_____

_____

_____

_____

_____

_____

_____

_____

_____

_____

PEACE IN THE *Middle* OF MESSES

SCRIPTURE

"He makes everything beautiful in its time."
– Ecclesiastes 3:11 (NIV)

DEVOTIONAL

The toys are everywhere, the dishes are stacked high, and your to-do list keeps growing. Your emotions feel just as scattered as your living room—stressed, stretched, and on the edge of tears. It's easy to think peace will only come when everything's finally in order. But God doesn't need a tidy space or a calm mood to show up. He's not overwhelmed by your mess—He's present in it. In fact, some of His most beautiful work happens in the middle of the chaos, not after it's cleaned up.

True peace isn't found in perfectly balanced schedules or Instagram-worthy homes—it's found in a heart surrendered to Jesus. When you let go of the pressure to fix everything and instead invite Him into the mess, He brings calm to your soul even if your surroundings stay loud and imperfect. He's building something holy right where you are, and His grace is more than enough to meet you in the middle of it all.

PRAYER

Jesus, I give You my messy life. Remind me that You're still creating beauty, even when things look unfinished. Amen.

REFLECTION

Where do you feel overwhelmed by mess right now? How might God be working in that place?

_____

_____

_____

_____

_____

_____

_____

_____

_____

_____

_____

_____

FINDING *Peace* IN FORGIVENESS

SCRIPTURE

"Be kind and compassionate to one another, forgiving each other, just as in Christ God forgave you." – Ephesians 4:32 (NIV)

DEVOTIONAL

Whether it's your child testing the same boundary again, a spouse's words that cut deep, or a friend who didn't show up when you needed them most—offenses hurt. And forgiveness can feel impossible, especially when trust has been broken or the pain lingers. But holding on to bitterness and resentment slowly drains your peace. It's a heavy weight to carry, and you weren't meant to bear it. Forgiveness doesn't mean pretending the hurt didn't matter. It means entrusting the pain to God and letting Him heal what you can't fix on your own.

God's grace is strong enough to carry you through the process. He never asks you to forgive in your own strength—He empowers you with His. Choosing forgiveness doesn't excuse the wrong; it sets your heart free from its grip. It's not about forgetting—it's about releasing. And in that release, peace has room to grow. Forgiveness may take time, but every step you take toward it is a step closer to the freedom Jesus died to give you.

PRAYER

God, help me forgive as You've forgiven me. Release the bitterness in my heart and fill the space with peace. Amen.

REFLECTION

Is there someone you need to forgive—or ask forgiveness from? What step could you take?

_____

_____

_____

_____

_____

_____

_____

_____

_____

_____

PEACE THAT PASSES *Understanding*

SCRIPTURE

"And the peace of God, which transcends all understanding, will guard your hearts and your minds in Christ Jesus." – Philippians 4:7 (NIV)

DEVOTIONAL

Sometimes peace just doesn't make sense. The diagnosis is still real. The bills are still due. The toddler is still screaming, and the job is still uncertain. And yet—your heart is steady. You're not unraveling. That kind of peace isn't something you can manufacture or explain—it's a gift straight from Jesus. His peace isn't fragile or dependent on good circumstances. It's strong enough to stand in the middle of chaos and keep your soul anchored.

Jesus never promised an easy life, but He did promise His presence. And with His presence comes a supernatural peace—one that guards your heart and mind like a shield. It doesn't always fix the problem or calm the storm, but it calms you. The world can't offer that kind of peace, and it can't take it away either. When everything around you says you should fall apart, His peace is what holds you together.

PRAYER

Jesus, thank You for a peace that defies logic. Guard my heart and mind today with Your presence. Amen.

REFLECTION

Where in your life are you desperate for peace? Ask Jesus to meet you right there.

_____
_____
_____
_____
_____
_____
_____
_____
_____
_____
_____

WHEN THE *World* FEELS HEAVY

SCRIPTURE

"I have told you these things, so that in me you may have peace. In this world you will have trouble. But take heart! I have overcome the world."
– John 16:33 (NIV)

DEVOTIONAL

The world feels heavy some days—wars, disasters, division, and personal heartbreak all swirl together until your spirit feels overwhelmed. Add in the weight of broken relationships or the pain of someone you love, and it's easy to feel crushed by it all. The sorrow around us is real, and as moms, we often carry it deeply. But Jesus never denied the reality of trouble—He acknowledged it and then gave us a powerful promise: *He has overcome the world.*

That truth changes everything. We don't have to ignore the pain or pretend things are fine. We can grieve with hope, cry with trust, and keep loving even when it's costly. Jesus' victory means darkness doesn't win. So today, let His peace steady you. Breathe deep. Turn off the noise if you need to. Rest in the truth that He is still on the throne—and because of that, you can keep going with courage and compassion, even in a broken world.

PRAYER

Jesus, when the world feels too heavy, lift my eyes to You. Thank You for being my peace in every storm. Amen.

REFLECTION

What worldly burden are you carrying? Surrender it to Jesus in prayer today.

_____

_____

_____

_____

_____

_____

_____

_____

_____

_____

_____

RESTORING *Wonder*

SCRIPTURE

"The heavens declare the glory of God; the skies proclaim the work of his hands." – Psalm 19:1 (NIV)

DEVOTIONAL

Children have a way of seeing the world that we often lose as adults. They marvel at bubbles floating in sunlight, bugs crawling in the grass, and bedtime stories told for the hundredth time. Their sense of wonder slows them down, opens their hearts, and roots them in the present moment. Somewhere along the way, we trade that wonder for worry, busyness, and distraction. But wonder isn't just childlike—it's holy. It reawakens peace by reminding us that beauty still exists, even in a chaotic world.

When you pause to notice a sunset, listen to your child's laughter, or feel the breeze through the window, you create space for peace to return. These small moments are whispers from God, pointing to His presence and His goodness. Wonder shifts your eyes from what's wrong to what's still right. And in that shift, you remember: He is still near, still good, and still inviting you to see the world through His eyes.

PRAYER

Creator God, open my eyes to wonder again. Let Your beauty break into my busy days and restore my peace. Amen.

REFLECTION

Where can you slow down today and notice something beautiful?

_____

_____

_____

_____

_____

_____

_____

_____

_____

_____

_____

LIVING IN *Lasting* PEACE

SCRIPTURE

"You will keep in perfect peace those whose minds are steadfast, because they trust in you."
– Isaiah 26:3 (NIV)

DEVOTIONAL

Peace isn't something you stumble into once and then keep forever without effort—it's a daily, sometimes moment-by-moment choice. As you close this devotional, know that the peace God offers isn't thin or breakable. It's deep and steady, anchored in who He is, not in how your day goes. You may still face messes, meltdowns, and moments of doubt—but peace can still rule your heart when Christ is at the center of it.

This peace doesn't mean everything makes sense or that life gets easier. It means you're never alone in the chaos. You have access to calm that surpasses understanding, to joy that outlasts sorrow, to strength made perfect in weakness. So keep showing up. Keep breathing deep. Keep choosing Jesus—again and again. His peace is not just possible; it's promised, and it's yours to carry forward.

PRAYER

Lord, thank You for walking with me through this year. Help me live rooted in Your peace, every single day. Amen.

REFLECTION

What has God taught you about peace through this journey?

_____

_____

_____

_____

_____

_____

_____

_____

_____

_____

_____

Closing Reflection & Blessing

You made it, mama. Fifty-two weeks of showing up, sometimes feeling weary, but always coming back to God, letting Him into the chaos of your everyday life. You've been intentional about choosing peace over perfection, about letting His voice be louder than the noise, and about trusting Him with the messiness of motherhood. It hasn't always been easy, but you've been faithful. And that faithfulness is seen by God.

You've embraced a truth that is so often overlooked: peace isn't about a perfect life—it's about a grounded life, rooted in God's love and grace, no matter the circumstances. You've chosen to find Him in the middle of the loud moments, the exhausting days, and the quiet whispers. You've invited Him in, and He has met you with the rest your soul needs.

As you walk forward, may you carry these truths with you:

You are not alone. In every moment, whether you feel seen or not, God is right there with you—holding you, guiding you, and walking beside you.

You are deeply loved. Not for what you do, not for how well you perform, but for who you are. You are God's beloved daughter, and His love for you is steadfast and unconditional.

You carry the peace of Christ within you. It's not a fleeting emotion, but a deep, lasting presence that calms your heart even in the stormiest of days. Wherever you go, you take His peace with you.

May the Lord bless you and keep you, mama. May His face shine upon you, lighting your path and filling you with the strength you need. May He give you peace—in every mess, every moment, and every miracle. No matter what today holds, you are held, you are loved, and you are enough. Amen.

About the Author

Rebecca graduated from Malone College in 2008 with a Bachelor's degree in Youth Ministry. She started writing & illustrating in 2013, about her dog Pookie, when she wanted a fun and wholesome story for her nieces and nephews, some of which were learning to read. She plans to keep up her series and write others. In 2019, she launched a publishing and entertainment company to help kids explore and nurture their creative side through books, tv shows, and art classes.

Along with *The Adventures of Pookie* children's book series, she is the illustrator of her sister, Megan Yee's books in the God's Books series. She is also the author of the personal development book *The Creative Minds Guide to Success*. She travels full time in a 5th wheel RV with her husband Eric, and their dog, Bailey, for his job as a Journeyman Lineman and writes about their adventures along the way.

Check out more:

God's Masterpiece

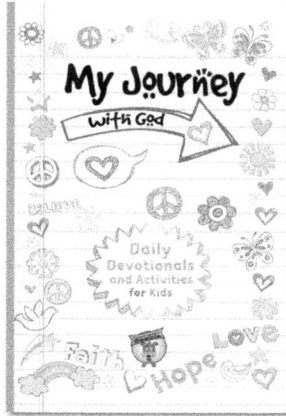
My Journey with God
Daily Devotionals and Activities for Kids
Faith Hope Love

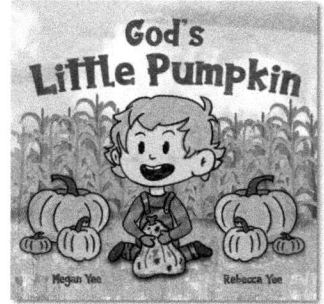
God's Little Pumpkin
Megan Yee   Rebecca Yee

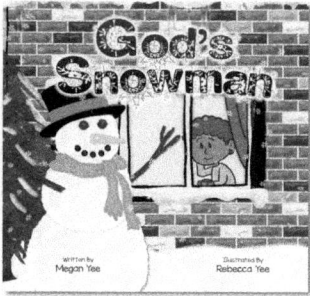
God's Snowman
Written By Megan Yee   Illustrated By Rebecca Yee

Love, Jesus

AdventuresOfPookie.com

The Adventures of Pookie LLC
ENTERTAINMENT

Books   Shows   Classes